Contents

Siula Grande

Introduction

This is the true story of two men
who set out to climb a mountain:
the dangers they faced on the way up,
and the disasters on the way down.

The two men were Simon Yates and Joe Simpson.

Joe had a fall, and broke his leg.
Simon tried a desperate rescue.
That rescue failed.
Simon had to leave his friend for dead
on the frozen mountain.

But Joe didn't die.
Joe and Simon both got back alive.
It sounds impossible, too good to be true.
But that's how it happened, in June 1985.

The mountain was Siula Grande,
in the Andes, in South America.

Joe Simpson and Simon Yates.

1 Base Camp

Simon Yates and Joe Simpson
arrived at the foot of the mountain in May 1985.
They made base camp at 4,500 metres
and got ready for the climb.

Siula Grande is 6,400 metres high.
No one had ever climbed the West Face before.
Simon and Joe wanted to be the first.

They had done a lot of climbing all over the world.
But these mountains were the biggest,
and highest, they had ever seen.

They were 120 kilometres from the nearest town,
two days' walk from the nearest road.
If anything went wrong, they were on their own.

They liked the idea of that freedom.
That danger.

This high in the mountains, nothing grows.
There's nothing but rocks and ice and snow.
You need crampons –
spikes on the toes and bottoms of your boots.
Without crampons,
Simon and Joe would slip and slide
hundreds of metres down to the waiting rocks.

You kick your crampons into the ice.
You hammer your ice axe in.
You hack little steps for your feet,
up a sheer wall of ice.
Step after step, hour after hour, for days.

That's all there is:
you and the thin air –
and the cruel mountain.

You need to be fit and strong –
and a little bit crazy –
to want to make this your life.

Base camp.

2 To the Top

They set off at five in the morning
on 4 June 1985.

Simon went first, cutting his way up the ice.
Joe followed, catching up quickly.
Then Joe climbed ahead, while Simon rested.

Then Simon went ahead.
Then Joe, and so on.

At mid-day they stopped for lunch –
some chocolate and some prunes!

Then they set off again.

When it got dark, they climbed in torch-light.
At 5,800 metres, they dug a snow-hole,
melted some ice to make tea, then had a sleep.

They had climbed non-stop for 15 hours.

Another day.
Only another 600 metres to go.

But steep snow was between them and the top.
They could see huge swirls of it,
like icing round the top of a cake.
Snow was more dangerous than ice –
they kept falling through it.
They had to go slowly, wading uphill,
up to their waists in snow.

It took six hours to climb the next 100 metres.
By 11 o'clock that night,
they were still 100 metres from the top.

They were tired, and cold.
It was –20° Centigrade,
even colder in the killing wind.
They could feel the frostbite in their fingers.

They dug another snow-hole and tried to sleep.

Next day, Simon and Joe took just a few hours
to get to the top.

It had taken weeks to get there,
and three days of hard climbing.
Now there was nowhere else to go.

They stood for a while in the sun,
filling up on chocolate, taking photos.

Then they began to look for a safe way down.

They knew they had to be careful.
Most climbing accidents happen on the way down.
You're more tired then, and not thinking.

It was then that the storm hit them.

The mountains during a snow storm.

3 The Break

In seconds, Simon and Joe were lost in storm-cloud.
Freezing wind and snow whipped them.
They couldn't see more than a metre ahead.

They stumbled and slipped and fell
– up to their eyes – in deep folds of snow.
Many times, they found a way down,
but then had to turn and climb back up
when they saw how dangerous that way was.

It took them a day and a night
to come down the first 300 metres.
It was their fourth night on the mountain.
The plan was to be back at base camp by now.
Instead, they had to dig another snow-hole.
They used the last of their gas
to cook the last of their food.

Next morning, in better weather,
Joe found a way down.

It was a little cliff of ice,
only 6 metres high.

All Joe had to do was climb down it.
After that, the way back to base camp
looked clear, and easy.

Carefully, slowly,
Joe made his way to the edge of the cliff.
He lay face down on the ice,
his feet over the edge.

He hammered his ice axes in
until he knew they'd take his weight.
Then he dropped his legs over the cliff-face
and kicked his crampons in.
He eased his weight on to his feet,
moved one ice axe nearer the edge,
then the other.

Joe was hanging upright on the cliff,
testing the ice for the next good hold –
when the ice broke away.

Joe fell backwards.

Before he could think or move,
Joe slammed into the slope
at the bottom of the cliff.

His legs jarred with the shock
and pain exploded in his right knee.

Joe fell back,
sliding head-first down the mountain on his back,
shouting out in shock and pain,
until the rope between him and Simon went tight,
and held, and stopped Joe's fall.

Joe tried to tell himself he was all right.
He tried to stand up,
to shake off the pain and panic he was feeling.
But waves of pain rushed up his right leg
and he fell back on the ice, gasping.

His leg was broken.
His shin had smashed up into his knee.
He could see the bone sticking out sideways.
There was no blood,
but he knew he was going to die.

'Are you okay?'
Simon had climbed down to where Joe lay.
'My leg,' Joe said. 'I think it's broken . . .'

Something changed in Simon's eyes.
He looked at Joe, then looked away.
Joe knew: Simon would leave him there
to die on the mountain – if he had to.

But now Simon was digging.
He dug a seat for himself in the snow.
It would hold him in place, he explained,
while he lowered Joe on the rope.

It might work.

Joe lay face down
and let himself slip down the slope,
until there was no more rope.
Then Simon climbed down to Joe.
They dug another seat in the snow,
and Joe slid another 100 metres closer to safety.

This happened nine or ten times.
Joe let himself think this might just work.

4 The Cut

All the way down,
Joe's leg smashed and jolted on every rock.
He screamed and swore up at Simon,
for letting him fall so fast.
In the storm, Simon didn't hear.

The slope was getting steeper.
Joe was heading over a cliff-face.
He screamed up at Simon again – 'Stop!'
Seconds later he was grabbing at the snow
as he slid over the edge of the cliff.
Then he was spinning in mid-air,
dangling in space on the end of the rope.

Simon didn't know what had happened. He went on
lowering Joe, until there was no more rope.

Joe tried to climb up, but his hands were too cold.
Simon was cold too. He had frostbite in his fingers.
He couldn't pull Joe back up. He could only hold on.

On the cliff-face.

They stayed like that for an hour and a half,
Simon wondering what had happened to Joe.

There were only two things that could happen next.
Either – Simon would get tired,
and Joe's weight would pull him off the mountain.
Or – Simon would cut the rope to save himself.
Either way, Joe would fall.

Joe looked down.
At the bottom of the cliff, 15 metres below him,
he could see a huge crack in the ice.
It was 6 metres wide.
If he fell, he would drop right into it.
Joe hung there, waiting to die.

Darkness fell, and froze around them.

Simon held on to the rope with frozen hands.
Then he remembered the knife in his rucksack.
He didn't have time to think. He grabbed it.
The rope was so tight, it sprang apart
as soon as the blade touched it.

Joe fell into the darkness.

5 The Crack in the Ice

After cutting the rope, Simon fell back and slept.
He knew Joe was dead,
broken on the rocks 300 metres below.
Simon was exhausted. He had frostbite.
He'd had no food or water for days.

He got back down to base camp as soon as he could.
When he was rested, and felt better,
he went out looking for Joe's body.

But Joe was not dead.
The agony in his leg told Joe he was not dead.

He woke up on a ledge,
inside the huge crack in the ice.
He had fallen into a shaft of ice,
a cold, dead, silent place.
Hard, white walls glistened blue
in the light of Joe's torch.
Far below him, darkness waited.

High above, beyond the hole he'd fallen through,
Joe could see the sky, and stars.

He pulled on the rope. It was his only chance,
his only link back to Simon, and safety.

The rope fell easily down into Joe's hands,
and kept on falling,
until the frayed end flicked past the light of the torch.
He stared at the frayed end, where Simon had cut it.

Joe sat back and sobbed.
He shouted and swore and sobbed
until he fell asleep.

When he woke up,
Joe tried climbing back up the ice walls,
back out through the hole at the top.

Impossible. He got a metre up,
then fell back on to the ledge,
landing on his broken leg.

As the pain died down,
he knew there was only one way out.

Joe fixed his last ice-screw to the wall,
fixed the rope to the ice-screw,
then lowered himself down into the darkness.

As he got lower down, the shaft opened out
into an ice cave, 15 metres across.
Joe's feet found the floor. But was it solid?
Maybe it was just a thin layer of snow . . .
Carefully, he stood on it. It held his weight.

On the far side of the ice cave,
12 metres away, was a long slope of snow.
It reached up 40 metres or more,
to the roof of the cave.
And in the roof, Joe could see – a little hole.
Daylight.

Joe started to think it out.
Could he crawl over to that slope?
Could he climb up, 40 metres,
with a badly broken leg?

He watched snow fall through the little hole,
watched it catch the sun as it fell.
He knew he had to try.

6 Daylight

Joe hacked little steps in the slope,
and hopped up them, one by one.
He tried to land on his good leg,
but time and time again, he landed badly
and stabbed his broken leg down into the snow.

The pain made him dizzy.
Then he had to stand on his broken leg,
to steady himself, to stop himself falling.

After five hours' climbing,
Joe was level with the little hole.
It was about the size of his head.
Joe skipped up on to the last little step he'd cut,
then poked his head out.

Blind, dazzling sunlight!

When he could see again,
Joe took a long look round.

The mountains had never looked so lovely.

Joe rolled out of the snow-hole,
and lay on the mountain-side in the sun.

The way down was clear.
He could see the ice-field
sweeping all the way down the mountain
to the jungle of rocks at the bottom.
Down there somewhere, just out of sight,
was base camp. So close now.

But Joe was exhausted.
He'd had no food, no water, for days.
He couldn't walk.
Base camp was ten kilometres away.
He'd never felt so small, and alone.
But he had to give it a try.

Joe dug his axes deep into the snow,
then dragged himself slowly downhill.

After two hours,
Joe found a line of footprints.
They were Simon's, heading down the mountain.

7 Crawling

Joe knew the footprints would lead him to safety.
He didn't feel so alone now.
Simon had been here – Simon was just ahead.

Joe crawled on all day,
dragging his right leg behind him.

He kept going by giving himself a target.
'See if you can get to that rock down there
in less than an hour.'
He tried not to rest.
He only stopped to check where he was,
and to warm the frostbite in his hands.

As night began to fall, the storms started again.
Joe was lashed with falling snow.
He dragged himself on, until it was too dark to see.

Then he dug a snow-hole
and waited for the storm to pass.

When Joe woke in the morning,
Simon's footprints were gone.

Lower down the mountain slopes
the ice was full of cracks and hidden drops.
Joe had to keep stopping and looking,
then dragging himself back up the ice,
hoping for a better way down.

At last, Joe slid off the edge of the ice,
and fell on to rocks.

He couldn't crawl this bit.
Some of the rocks were as big as a house.
He couldn't slide along, like he could over the ice.
He had to learn to hop, and stumble and fall,
hop, stumble and fall, to keep himself moving.

With every step, every fall,
Joe stabbed his bad leg on to rock.
He screamed out in pain.
Then he decided to stop screaming all the time.
It didn't help – it didn't make the pain go away.
He strapped his sleeping mat round his leg –
like a splint – and carried on stumbling down.

As he got closer to home,
Joe tried to remember where he was.
Had he seen this lake before? That gully?
Wasn't it near the tents at base camp?

But he'd had no food or water for days.
His mind was playing tricks.
He saw people who weren't there.
He saw his mum and friends in the pub at home.
Joe chatted with them.
He sang pop songs, over and over again,
until they drove him crazy.
He kept on going.

Joe spent another night out under the stars.
He tried not to fall asleep.
He knew he was so cold, he might not wake up.

Joe lay awake for hours, fighting his fears.
He didn't want to face what he was thinking.
Base camp was so close now.
But what if Simon wasn't there?
Simon thought that Joe was dead.
So why would he want to wait around?
What if Joe got there, and Simon had already gone?

There was no time to lose.
It was quarter to one in the morning
when Joe set off again, stumbling and crawling.

Soon, he needed to rest.
He sat with his back against a rock.
It took him a long time to work out where he was,
and what the smell was.

He looked down. His gloves were covered with . . .
what was it? What *was* that smell . . .?

Joe had crawled into their toilet,
right on the edge of base camp.

He got himself upright, one last time.
He stared into the blackness.
Couldn't see a thing.

What if Simon had gone?

Joe called into the night:

'SIMON!'

8 Home

A light came on.
Joe saw a tent in front of him.
Then he heard the sounds of someone waking.

'Joe? Joe? Is that you?'

Thank God. Thank God.
Joe fell back on to the rocks.

Simon found him, and dragged him into the tent.
It was warm, and there was food, and tea.
Pain-killers.

Amazed, they both told their side of the story.
Joe had something important he needed to say:

'You did the right thing, Simon.
You did what you had to do.'

'Thank you!'

Joe Simpson on the mountain slopes.

Joe had spent a week on the mountain.
He'd lost over 3 stones (19 kilograms) in weight.

He'd broken his heel, as well as his knee.
When Simon found him,
Joe's leg was starting to smell of gangrene.

It took two days to get him to hospital.
It was another two days
before the doctors operated on him.

Joe started a diary while he was in hospital.
He was trying to make sense of what had happened.

Some time later, Joe got his diary out again,
and wrote the full story.

He called his book *Touching the Void*.
It was a best-seller all over the world.
A film – also called *Touching the Void* –
came out in 2003.

Joe dedicated the book to Simon Yates.